REAL-LIFE MONSTERS
CREEPY, CRAWLY CREATURES

THE WORLD'S WEIRDEST SPIDERS AND BUGS

Thanks to the creative team:
Senior Editor: Alice Peebles
Designer: Lauren Woods and collaborate agency

Original edition copyright 2015 by Hungry Tomato Ltd.

Hungry Tomato™
A division of Lerner Publishing Group, Inc.
241 First Avenue North
Minneapolis, MN 55401 USA

For reading levels and more information, look up this title
at www.lernerbooks.com.

Main body text set in Century Gothic Regular 9.5/11.5
Typeface provided by Monotype Corporation

Library of Congress Cataloging-in-Publication Data

The Cataloging-in-Publication Data for *Creepy, Crawly Creatures* is
on file at the Library of Congress.

ISBN 978-1-4677-6362-2 (lib. bdg.)
ISBN 978-1-4677-7642-4 (pbk.)
ISBN 978-1-4677-7226-6 (EB pdf)

Manufactured in the United States of America
1 – VP – 7/15/15

REAL-LIFE MONSTERS
CREEPY, CRAWLY CREATURES

By Matthew Rake

Illustrated by Simon Mendez

HUNGRY
TOMATO™

Minneapolis

CONTENTS

Small is beautiful, they say. But that's not necessarily so in the animal kingdom.

Welcome to the world of tiny terrors and mini-monsters. Don't let their size fool you. They are some of the most fearsome, poisonous, and downright revolting creatures on Earth.

Take the green-banded broodsac. It's a flatworm and it's quite obnoxious. It spends its entire life crawling around the insides of snails or birds. The only time it sees the outside world is when it is slithering around in bird poo! The tongue-eating louse *(right)* is just as bad. The female louse lives in a fish's mouth, and it actually takes the place of the fish's tongue.

Animals like these are known as parasites, which means they benefit at the expense of other animals. One of the most devious parasites is the emerald jewel wasp. It picks on the cockroach and uses it to raise its young. The wasp's larvae literally eat the roach alive, and the roach can do absolutely nothing about it.

Other tiny animals are highly toxic. The Indian red scorpion is only the size of a tube of lip balm, but it has enough venom to kill a human. The bullet ant has the most painful sting of any insect. The pain has been likened to what it feels like to be shot. Perhaps most scary of all is the Asian giant hornet. When it is not trashing honeybee hives, it's targeting humans—and killing them.

Some of these tiny terrors are really sneaky. The tarantula sets up trip wires with its silk to catch prey. Assassin bugs *(left)* and praying mantises imitate flowers and leaves before attacking their prey. And the Amazonian centipede *(below)* has a smart way of killing bats: it hangs from the ceiling of caves and catches them mid-flight.

So if you think small is beautiful, don't read any more—because we'll show you that small can be very, very dangerous.

GREEN-BANDED BROODSAC

Lenght: Various
Location: Europe and
North America

The green-banded broodsac is a flatworm, which is not the most sophisticated animal on Earth. It has no skeleton. It takes in oxygen but has no organs, such as lungs or gills, to help it breathe. It usually has an opening for taking in food, but it is exactly the same opening through which it poos!

However, in one respect, the green-banded broodsac is very clever. It has a smart way of making sure it reproduces so its species stays alive. It spends nearly all its life inside the body of a snail or a bird.

1 The green-banded broodsac starts life as an egg in a bird. The bird poops out the egg and, after it lands on the ground or a tree branch, it gets eaten by a snail, nature's vacuum cleaner.

The snail can't digest the egg. So after living in the snail's gut for a short while, the broadsac egg develops into a miracidium (larva).

2 The miracidium wanders around the snail's body and changes into a sporocyst. This long tubelike form then enters through the back of the snail's eyestalk. The sporocyst stretches out the eyestalk and changes the it to green and yellow. For any bird that happens to be flying overhead, the snail's eyes now look like delicious morsels of caterpillar meat. The sporocyst even pulsates at a rate of 60 to 80 times a minute to attract a bird's attention.

3 Most birds would normally never go near a yucky snail. But they will gobble up the irresistible caterpillar-like eyestalks. Once swallowed by a bird, the broodsac develops into an adult while feeding off the food the bird eats. And, of course, it will also reproduce, sending out a stream of eggs to be pooped out by the bird. If the poop is eaten by another unsuspecting snail, the cycle starts again!

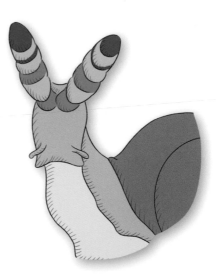

SIZE	1
POWER	2
STRENGTH	2
AGGRESSION	2
DEADLINESS	2
TOTAL	**9**

9 THE CREEPY CRUSTACEAN

TONGUE-EATING LOUSE

Length: 0.3 - 1.1 in (8–29 mm)

Location: off the coast of Central and South America

Open wide! Can you see the louse inside that red snapper fish? That's where it likes to live. There it is safe and can raise its young. The red snapper can't be too happy about it, though. The louse has eaten its tongue and is now attached to the snapper's mouth instead.

This is the only known example of an animal replacing another animal's body part, a story that will really get tongues wagging.

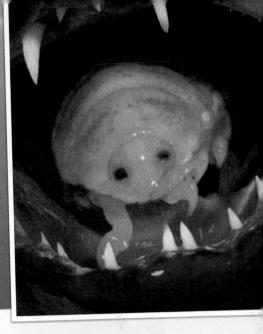

A MOTHER LOUSE IN MY MOUTH!

The tongue-eating louse is not actually a louse, but a type of crustacean like crabs, lobsters, barnacles, and shrimp. But this crustacean is different! Not only is it a blood-sucker that makes its home in a fish's mouth. It also has the ability to change from male to female .

It begins life as a juvenile male trying to get into the gills of a fish. For some reason, it really likes red snappers, but it will also try this with other fish. If other lice arrive at the gills though, the first louse will turn into a female and crawl up through the fish's throat to the mouth. There, it attaches its seven pairs of legs to the base of the fish's tongue. It then digs its five jaws into the main part of the tongue. It feeds off the fish's tongue. After all, it's the tastiest part!

The next stage in the louse's life is a little mysterious. Scientists think the female louse may mate with one of the males in the gills. Experts aren't sure, but they think the louse's young are released into the water when the fish is in a school with other fish. That way, the young lice have a better chance of finding other fish to latch on to. And if a juvenile louse finds a fish, the cycle can begin again. Turn to page 28 to see what happens to the adult louse and the fish.

SIZE	3
POWER	3
STRENGTH	3
AGGRESSION	5
DEADLINESS	4
TOTAL	18

Length: Females - up to 5 in (13 cm);
Males - up to 4 in (10 cm)
Location: East Africa

The praying mantis gets its name from the way it holds its forelegs: like the arms of a person praying. But in this pose, the mantis is not at rest. It is ready to pounce on its prey. Should a fly, a moth, a butterfly, or a beetle stray into view, the mantis will swiftly seize the insect between the sharp spines on its forelegs. With the prey held firmly in its legs, the mantis can bite off pieces with its jaws.

Flower mantises, such as this devil's flower mantis, are extra clever. They disguise themselves as flowers, stalks, and leaves *(left)*, so no prey will see them before being caught.

NOT GREAT MATES

As with other species of mantis, the female devil's flower mantis will often eat the male after mating, or even during mating. She usually goes for the head first! Even if the male loses his head (literally) in the process of mating, he can still complete the act. Some male mantises try to interest the female in a courtship dance to change her focus from feeding to mating!

ASSUME THE POSE

When threatened by a hungry bird or a lizard, the devil's flower praying mantis tries to look bigger and scarier than it really is. It raises its front legs above its head and opens them wide in what is called a deimatic display. It uses the pose to scare off predators or simply to distract them so it can make a quick getaway.

SIZE

6

POWER

3

STRENGTH

3

AGGRESSION

4

DEADLINESS

3

TOTAL

19

LYING IN WAIT

ASSASSIN BUGS

Length: 0.4 - 1.2 in (1 - 3 cm)
Location: Worldwide

There are thousands of species of assassin bugs. Some of them kill animals that are a nuisance to us, such as bed bugs, flies, mosquitoes, and wasps as well as garden pests, such as caterpillars and beetles.

Other assassin bugs are not quite as helpful. The kissing bug comes out at night and often bites people around the mouth while they sleep. In Central and South America, it spreads the deadly Chagas disease this way!

1. The milkweed assassin bug lives in North, Central, and South America. It uses a "sticky trap" strategy. It hides inside foliage with its forelegs raised in the air. These are covered with a glue-like substance that traps prey.

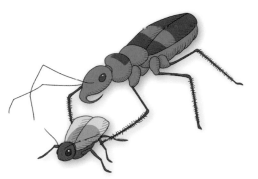

2. Once the prey is captured, the milkweed assassin quickly punctures the body of its victim and pumps in toxic saliva. Then it sucks up the insides of its prey as if it were enjoying a drink through a straw.

3. The bug can feed on prey up to six times its own size. But the bigger the prey, the longer it takes to feed—and this means it becomes more vulnerable to other predators. So if it's too greedy, it might get eaten while it's having dinner!

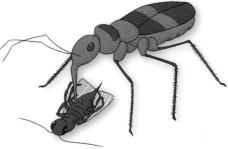

SIZE

3

POWER

2

STRENGTH

2

AGGRESSION

6

DEADLINESS

7

TOTAL

20

RED ASSASSIN BUG

The red assassin bug is common in Europe. It is about 0.8 inches (2 centimeters) long and preys on spiders and insects, including bees and wasps. Its sting can be more painful than a bee's. So if you see one, don't touch it!

BEAUTY OR BEAST?

EMERALD JEWEL WASP

6

Length: up to 0.86 in (22 mm)
Location: South and Southeast Asia, Africa, and the Pacific Islands

Zombie cockroaches! It might sound like one of the weirdest science fiction films out there—but they really do exist. The emerald jewel wasp turns cockroaches into helpless, zombified creatures to make sure its eggs turn into adults.

If you think this wasp, with its shimmering shades of blue and green, looks stunningly beautiful, remember it's a deadly enemy—for cockroaches. Who would ever think you could feel sorry for a cockroach?

1. When the female wasp is ready to lay her eggs, she finds a cockroach and stings it twice. This first sting temporarily paralyzes the roach's front legs. The second one zombifies the cockroach. It can feel everything but can't act on its own.

2. Next, the wasp grips the roach's antennae and leads it to a burrow. It is almost as if the wasp is taking a dog out for walk on a leash. The roach, in its zombified state, walks perfectly normally and fully cooperates.

3. Once inside the burrow, the wasp lays her egg on the cockroach's underside. The wasp's work is now done and she can fly off in search of new roaches.

4. After a few days, the egg hatches and the larva chews its way into the roach's abdomen. It stays there for the next week, eating the roach's internal organs. The roach dies, and the larva changes into a pupa inside the roach's dead body. It spins a cocoon and grows eyes, legs, and wings. After about a month, it is ready to fly.

SIZE
3

POWER
2

STRENGTH
2

AGGRESSION
6

DEADLINESS
8

TOTAL
21

TOP GUN

BULLET ANT

Length: up to 1 in (25 mm)
Location: Rainforests of Central
and South America

What's the most painful insect sting on the planet? The common wasp or the honeybee? Not even close. The sting of the tarantula hawk wasp is a contender. But the most painful of all is that of the bullet ant. According to human victims, its sting feels like being shot, and that's how the ant got its name. One person described the pain like this: "It's like fire-walking over flaming charcoal with a 3-inch (7.6-cm) rusty nail in your heel."

RITE OF PASSAGE

In some parts of the world, it takes a lot to become a man. When boys of the Sateré-Mawé tribe in Brazil reach the age of 13, they collect bullet ants. A medicine man sedates the insects with an herbal solution and then weaves them inside a pair of gloves. A boy must wear the gloves for a full 10 minutes without screaming. Remember, one ant's sting is like being shot by a gun, and there are loads of ants woven into the gloves.

SIZE

4

POWER

4

STRENGTH

3

AGGRESSION

8

DEADLINESS

7

TOTAL

26

4 BIG, HAIRY, AND SCARY

TARANTULA

Length: 1 - 4 in (2.5 - 10 cm)
with leg span of 3 - 12 in (8 - 30 cm)
Location: warm regions worldwide

Tarantulas don't use webs to capture prey like other spiders do. They do it the hard way: on foot. But, a web wouldn't be much use in trapping some of the animals that tarantulas like to eat. Their diet includes frogs, mice, birds, and even snakes.

PARALYZING ITS PREY

A tarantula usually hunts at night, sneaking up on prey and pouncing! It has fangs like a doctor's needle. With each bite, it injects venom through its fangs into its victim—in this case, a tree frog. The venom paralyzes the prey. The tarantula the injects digestive juices from its mouth into the body of its prey. These juices turn the frog into a soupy mess that the spider can easily slurp up.

SIZE

6

POWER

5

STRENGTH

5

AGGRESSION

6

DEADLINESS

5

TOTAL

27

A STING IN THE TALE

INDIAN RED SCORPION

Length: 2 - 3.5 in (5 - 9 cm)
Location: India, Pakistan, Nepal, Sri Lanka

The Indian red might not look like the scariest scorpion around. It is only the size of a tube of lip balm, about half as big as the world's largest scorpions. But the Indian red is a real toxic terror.

One sting can cause humans excruciating pain, vomiting, breathlessness, convulsions, and sometimes major heart problems. Oh, and if that isn't enough, it can also turn a victim's skin blue and make them froth at the mouth with pink, slimy mucus. Without receiving urgent treatment, a person can die.

Some scientists think that the death rate from bites of the Indian red scorpion is as high as 40%. The good news is that, like other scorpions, it is actually a very shy creature. However, it will attack if disturbed, and it often finds its way into houses. Since people in Asia often wear sandals or go barefoot, the scorpion usually finds some nice, exposed skin to sting.

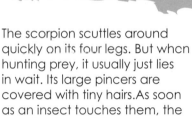

The scorpion scuttles around quickly on its four legs. But when hunting prey, it usually just lies in wait. Its large pincers are covered with tiny hairs. As soon as an insect touches them, the scorpion jumps into action.

The Indian red goes for the kill with its pincers first. If thas doesn't work, it has a sting in its tail. The end of the scorpion's tail is called the telson. It contains a pair of venom glands and a barb that injects the venom. WIth the prey held in its pincers, the scorpion curls its tail over its body to deliver the sting to the prey.

Since the scorpion eats food in liquid form only, it cuts off a small amount of the prey with its very sharp mouth parts, known as chelicerata (cheh-lee-seh-rah-tah). It vomits digestive juices to dissolve the insides of its prey. The scorpion can then suck in the liquid meal.

SIZE

5

POWER

5

STRENGTH

5

AGGRESSION

4

DEADLINESS

9

TOTAL

28

A LONG STORY

AMAZONIAN GIANT CENTIPEDE

Length: 12 in (30 cm)
Location: Northern South America, Caribbean

Can you imagine this centipede creeping across the forest floor, moving its legs in a wavelike rhythm in search of a tasty meal? It feeds on almost everything it can kill, including small lizards, snakes, mice, and bats. The centipede is longer than an adult's forearm but some of its prey is even bigger. So what is the reason behind its hunting success? Well, it has a secret weapon: a pair of sharp claws at the front of its body. These are known as forcipules and they hold deadly venom, which leaves its prey paralyzed.

DO CENTIPEDES HAVE 100 LEGS?

No. A centipede has one pair of legs on each section of its body and it always has an odd number of sections. It might have 49 sections and 98 legs or 51 sections and 102 legs.

The Amazonian giant centipede has either 21 or 23 sections, so it has 42 or 46 legs.

SIZE
8
POWER
5
STRENGTH
6
AGGRESSION
5
DEADLINESS
7
TOTAL
31

SNAKE-EATER

Often a snake will prey on a centipede, but occasionally a centipede will manage to eat a snake. Sometimes the centipede is half the weight of the snake. But if it can inject its venom near the snake's head, it will overpower it.

1 THE DEADLY WASP

ASIAN GIANT HORNET

Length: 2 in (50 mm)
Location: Eastern Asia

Who's scared of a hornet? Sure, they might give you a painful sting but they are not going to kill you, are they? Wrong. The Asian giant hornet is a real monster. It's the world's largest hornet, with a wingspan of 3 inches (76 millimeter). That's as wide as a baseball. And with its 0.24-inch (6-mm) stinger, it delivers a deadly venom that can kill a human. And it kills many people every year, especially in Japan.

HAVING A BALL

Giant hornets love to attack honeybee hives and they usually create complete carnage. One hornet can tear up about 40 honeybees every minute, leaving a pile of severed heads and wings in its wake. However, Japanese honeybees have an amazing defensive strategy. Hundreds of them will swarm over the hornet intruder and hold it in a tight ball. When its internal temperature rises to 117°F (47°C), the hornet roasts to death.

4	POWER
7	STRENGTH
6	AGGRESSION
9	DEADLINESS
8	
TOTAL	
34	

GREEN-BANDED BROODSAC

Snails infected with the green-banded broodsac tend to come out in the open. Scientists believe the broodsac takes control of the snail's brain and forces it into the open. Why? It is easier for birds to see them and eat them!

TONGUE-EATING LOUSE

Once the female louse has released her young from inside the fish's mouth, her job is done. She either floats away or gets swallowed by the fish. The fish's fate is sealed as it cannot survive without a tongue!

EMERALD JEWEL WASP

The emerald wasp is a solitary wasp and, like all other adult wasps, is unable to eat solid food. It relies on sucking or drinking the hemolymph (blood) of cockroaches and other insects.

BULLET ANT

Bullet ants live in large colonies containing up to several hundred individuals. They usually build nests with chambers that have domed ceilings at the bottom of tall trees. Often the chamber walls are lined with plant matter that the worker ants have foraged.

AMAZONIAN GIANT CENTIPEDE

The Amazonian centipede is the longest centipede on Earth, but it's nowhere near the leggiest. The *Gonibregmatus plurimipes* from Fiji in the Pacific Ocean has 382 legs! The leggiest creature of all is a millipede. The *Illacme plenipes* lives in California and, at 1.2 inches (3 cm), is much smaller than your little finger. But the females still manage to have up to 750 legs.

DEVIL'S FLOWER PRAYING MANTIS

The praying mantis is the only invertebrate (animal without a backbone) to be able to see in 3D. They have five eyes—two large ones and three smaller ones in between.

ASSASSIN BUG

A West African assassin bug carries the remains of the ants, termites, and flies it has eaten on its back—a "backpack" of carcasses. If a predator tries its luck, it is likely to end up with a mouthful of dead insects instead of the assassin bug.

TARANTULA

After mating, female tarantulas lay hundreds of eggs and encase them in a silken sac that they spin. They guard the eggs aggressively and occasionally turn them over with their jaws to help brood them. If distressed, however, they sometimes eat the eggs.

INDIAN RED SCORPION

Scorpions are among the oldest land animals, dating back about 400 million years. The first scorpions, however, were sea scorpions. Closely related to the land variety, they could grow to an amazing 8 feet (2.5 meters) long and had vicious claws the size of tennis rackets.

ASIAN GIANT HORNET

Giant hornets tend to attack honeybee nests in autumn when they are rearing queens and males in their nests. After a successful attack, the hornets will chew up the bodies of the honeybee larvae and pupae and take them back to their hive to feed to their own larvae. Hornet workers retrieve food from the honeybee hive for up to two weeks.

ALL IN A DAY'S WORK

In bullet-ant society, smaller workers stay inside the nest and tend to the queen and her eggs, while larger ones forage and defend the nest. The foragers often venture as far up as the canopy—130 feet (40 m) above ground. There they collect nectar, the sugar-rich liquid produced by plants and some small insects such as termites, other smaller ants, and even wasps.

These ants take the food back to the nest in their mandibles, a pair of clawlike limbs near their mouth. They can even carry liquid droplets without bursting them. Everything is shared with other ants and larvae inside the nest.

WILY WAYS

Assassin bugs use some very crafty hunting strategies. An Australian assassin bug will hang out in a spider's web, plucking the strands. When the spider comes to see if it caught some prey, the spider becomes the prey for the assassin bug.

A Costa Rican assassin bug hunts termites. It knows that termites will remove dead individuals from the nest to keep it disease-free. Once the assassin bug has caught one termite and sucked it dry, it dangles the termite's remains into the termite nest. When another termite comes to clear up the dead body, the assassin bug captures a new victim. One assassin bug was seen using this trick to capture 48 termites in a single sitting!

CENTIPEDES OR MILLIPEDES?

Centipedes and millipedes are both myriapods. So what's the difference between them? The main difference is that millipedes have two pairs of legs on each section of their body, while centipedes have just one pair on each section. Millipedes also tend to feed off decaying plant matter, whereas nearly all centipedes (such as the Amazonian giant) are predators. As a result, centipedes generally move more quickly because they have to chase prey.

The oldest known land animal, *Pneumodesmus newmani*, was a myriapod that lived 428 million years ago. And if you think the Amazonian giant centipede is a good size at 12 inches (30 cm), that's nothing compared to the arthropleura millipede. It lived around 320 million years ago and measured 8.5 feet (2.6 m): as long as two full-size bicycles!

THE HUMAN KILLER

The giant hornet is certainly not afraid of humans. Each year in Japan, it kills around 30 to 40 people. In 2013 in China, it killed at least 42 people and injured more than 1,600 others. One victim told the local media: "The more you run, the more they want to chase you." And some victims described being chased for more than 650 feet (200 m). The giant hornet is fast, too; it can fly up to 25 miles per hour (40 km/h).

However, humans do get their own revenge. The hornet is a delicacy in mountain villages in Japan, eaten either raw (hornet sashimi) or deep fried. Bon appétit!

INDEX

THE AUTHOR

Matthew Rake lives in London, England, and has worked in publishing for more than twenty years. He has written on a wide variety of topics including science, sports, and the arts.

THE ARTIST

Award-winning illustrator Simon Mendez combines his love of nature and drawing by working as an illustrator with a focus on scientific and natural subjects. He paints on a wide variety of themes but mainly concentrates on portraits and animal subjects. He lives in the United Kingdom.